How To Be An Effective Cop: A Quick Guide For Non Readers
Exclusively & internationally sold on Amazon.

This book is blunt and touches on some uncomfortable truths for people. However, in order to be a productive part of law enforcement, you must have the ability to handle the things we'll discuss. This book is meant to be quick, but also provoke your thinking. If you come across a topic you're unfamiliar with, please be resourceful and search for additional resources to help further your understanding. Most people remain uninformed because they hate reading, but National Public Radio (NPR, local listings available on their website), videos, podcasts, and audio books are other ways you can learn things. Law enforcement is an arena that involves a wide variety of skills and people. The more you know and understand about life in general, the better you'll be at your job. At the end of this book are random helpful sources for you to explore and expand your knowledge. Most of us pride ourselves in knowing things, but we can't actually know things without intaking the knowledge. Sometimes we forget this basic fact and operate based on uneducated assumptions.

In order to gain the most out of this book, it's best to read it with a learning mentality. You can't learn if you can't acknowledge you have something to gain. Don't assume you know best or that you are already well developed. Just be open, allow yourself to think, and ask questions. If you find yourself getting defensive, pause and correct yourself. If you stay in defense mode, that means you're not learning or evolving, but trying your hardest to remain the same. Most of the time, people are either offended by my direct presentation, they're unwilling to accept the truth, or they confuse the point being made with their incorrect assumptions. If you get offended by what you read, try to find exactly why you feel that way. Our emotions or ego can make it hard to see things for what they are and defensiveness can get the best of us. To help avoid that, I recommend frequently questioning 'why.' For example, why do I feel this way, why would someone say that, or why is this my perception. I also recommend being as critical of yourself as you would a stranger. For example, ask yourself if you would accept a stranger having your same explanations or behaviors.

Most departments don't require an adult education so it's important you understand a major dynamic that exists. For years, studies have shown officers who are college educated are less likely to have misconduct issues than those who are not. This includes use of excessive force and violating policy. This should make you question why, especially if you're uneducated. College isn't just a place where people learn an area of knowledge for a degree. For successful (*key word*) students, a lot happens in those years which amounts to them developing a thorough thought process and self-awareness. Developing a thorough thought process and self-awareness require deliberate effort. They don't automatically develop as we age, as maturity usually does. You don't have to go to college to develop them because I am giving you a few tools to start the process. Don't assume you will be an officer who won't have misconduct issues. The officers who do have issues probably assumed they wouldn't either. Instead, understand it's a possibility and think of this guide as your tool to deliberately prevent such a scenario.

Enjoy, pass it on, & post on social media!

Bigot Stain

The harsh reality of law enforcement is, it started with corruption and immorality. That is an indisputable fact that is forever etched in America's public record. Racism, sexism, and all forms of bigotry are what law enforcement openly thrived in. All while maintaining the image of standing for justice and protecting people. You need to understand this because it is relevant today. It doesn't matter how well you view law enforcement, that will never outweigh the history. Nor will it outweigh the current data that shows corruption and bigotry are still intertwined in this profession. There are a lot of bad officers, too many for the type of noble profession policing is. To add, there are a lot of cops who aren't directly bad, but they're complicit and therefore no better.

Much of the public already knows the unfavorable history. Now that you know it, understand, no matter how good of a cop you are, your badge has always represented contradiction. It's not productive to downplay that or act like it's no longer a relevant issue. Nor is it productive to act as though the badge automatically means you're a good person or cop. Instead, embrace this harsh reality and strive to do better. People aren't going to be inclined to trust you if you can't acknowledge the reality they already know exists. How can you possibly be different if you can't acknowledge the basics?

Truly understanding what this means will change how you interact with people who hate or fear what you represent. I was raised in the hood and hated cops. During college I learned how to get over that hate, but it took years of deliberate work. Many of the people you encounter who dislike you, won't have that much thought about it. This is where the meaning of professional comes in for you. Professional doesn't just refer to how spiffy and clean-cut you look. It's about how you conduct yourself, especially in moments of conflict. If you cannot control your emotions when provoked, you're not the professional your badge says you are. Their distrust for you is valid and your distrust for them is valid. The difference is, you're a trained professional with insight. You have the knowledge and capabilities to keep your encounters calm. Another difference is, law enforcement gave themself the bad image to begin with, so law enforcement has to take the initiative to fix it.

The first time I encountered a cop hating citizen while on duty, my self-awareness immediately came in to play. The moment I approached him I was polite and treated him with respect. He was rude and disrespectful. I intended on giving him only a warning, but he didn't give two f**ks about it. Rather than be offended or retaliate with my authority over him, I immediately thought to myself, 'I understand him because I was him years ago.' Not only could I relate, but I understood his anger toward me was valid because of the history my badge represented. As rude as he was, he didn't display any threatening behavior. I stayed respectful to him and I gave him my warning as intended, nothing more. Sure I had the discretion to cite him, but as a professional I don't play childish games where I one-up people because I'm upset they don't like me. People are within their rights to be rude to you. Don't be that officer who mistakes dislike for a crime.

Look In The Mirror

You already have many of the answers for how you need to be as an officer. Although we generally distinguish between citizens and officers, don't let this confuse you. You're a normal citizen. You are literally of the same population as the people you're supposed to protect. Also among the people you're supposed to protect are the bad people, your loved ones, and the loved ones of your fellow officers. You generally don't know who is who, but you know how you want to be treated by an unknown officer when you're off duty. You also know how you want your loved ones to be treated. BE THE COP YOU EXPECT UNDER THOSE CIRCUMSTANCES. It's that simple. Don't be the cop who is out of touch with reality and automatically sees a suspect in anyone not in a uniform. If you notice this start to happen with you, take a step back and correct yourself. If you walk around viewing everyone as a suspect or enemy, you will see and make trouble where there isn't any. That's delusion and it's dangerous. Is the goal of an officer to be a threat to people or protect them?

You have a valid reason to be cautious of people given the nature of your job. Remember though, people also have a valid reason to be cautious of you, given the history and current practices of law enforcement. I always cringe when I hear an officer justify certain behavior with, 'I have to make sure I go home at night.' That is essentially saying their duty is to protect their own life by any means necessary because only their life matters. Yes, we have to make sure we go home at night, but isn't that the goal of most people, not just officers? By taking an oath to protect people, you're also saying you have a duty to make sure citizens go home at night. Your concern for making it home doesn't give you the pass to recklessly act based on your assumptions, rather than according to the situation at hand. If your idea of self preservation automatically means trouble for citizens, the whole purpose of your job is defeated.

No matter your religion, race, or demographics, if you were raised in America, you were raised in a culture of bigotry. How we speak, the language of our laws, our neighborhoods, our practices, and all of our surroundings are glaring examples. The only reason many people are blind to them is because this is our everyday life and it's what we are accustomed to. As humans, we are naturally going to be products of our environment. Unless you never left your house nor mingled with other people, you are some type of product of American culture. People often reject the idea of being a product of bigotry because they feel they're a nice person or were 'raised right.' Although those things matter, they don't outweigh all the varying ways you've been exposed to American culture. To be clear, bigotry doesn't always look like hate or violence. Sometimes it's a matter of simply being naive and confusing your beliefs with facts.

As an example, let's look at the term emotional. American culture says women are emotional and men generally aren't. Many of us can support this idea by recalling countless examples of women crying and men remaining stone face. Seems like an indisputable fact right? As convincing as our life examples seem, it's not a fact that women are emotional and men aren't. What is a fact is, we've come to accept emotional as a term that refers to emotions women typically display more often, while ignoring the emotions more typically displayed by men. It's also a term generally directed at anyone seen as more feminine, regardless of the emotion they're displaying. Emotional doesn't specifically mean an extreme or outward display of emotion, nor does it refer to only negative emotions. It can mean those things, but in general it means relating to emotion of any kind. Fear, disgust, happiness, and surprise are examples of emotions.

One example of emotion people often disregard is the anger typically displayed by men. Yes, anger is an emotion and it's a very significant one. The vast majority of violent crimes are committed by men. The majority of street crimes are committed by men who come from backgrounds which often produce a lot of destructive emotions in people. Men may not be prone to crying, but committing crimes and violence are emotional displays. The fact is, humans, male and female, are emotional creatures and everything we do directly or indirectly ties back to an emotion. The people who aren't emotional have certain disorders which affect their emotional capabilities.

I know some people are indifferent to the ideas we've discussed, so I have some questions for you. What is your purpose for being in law enforcement? Do you think you're a good person? Do you think you're a good officer? If you can honestly answer yes to the last two and your first response has something to do with helping people, serving the community, or cleaning up the streets, then good. Even if you answered yes to the last questions, but became an officer for other reasons, that's still good. However, if you're indifferent to what has been discussed or don't care to actually work on your self or the issues, how does that align with your responses to the questions? How are you serving the community or being a good person/cop if you're ignoring major problems of the community and law enforcement? If someone said they cared about you, but never made an effort to see or talk with you and were indifferent to your problems, what would you take that to mean? Saying you're a good cop or person means absolutely nothing. Actually being one does.

For the few reading this who are corrupt or bigots, why point the finger at others for being lawless or immoral if you're exactly what you accuse them of? There are plenty of guilty people committing offenses who need to be stopped? Why waste time unjustly going after certain people simply because your uneducated bias toward them, tells you they're always guilty? If you're bitter at the world because of your own life traumas and are projecting, you would be less angry and burdened with revenge if you just worked on addressing those personal issues. From someone who knows, it feels more fulfilling to be a better person than the people who caused you trouble. If you're just stuck in your ways because that's the way you were raised, your inability to evolve with the times is a major characteristic of low intelligence. You can't see it, but everyone else can.

Outdated Community Policing

Community policing is now a part of most departments in the country. However, there tends to be a big disconnect. Community policing is important for the entire community, but where you really have to put in effort and thought is with the people who don't like you. Why does it matter? Besides the fact they're part of the community too, think in terms of your safety and job. You never know when you'll have to rely on them for information or to save your life. <u>Not everyone who dislikes you is a threat to your safety</u>, but the people who are a threat to your safety are often among those who dislike you.

Whether you feel anxiety, fear, an adrenaline rush, anger, or anything other than calm, the population who doesn't like you is probably one of the most difficult areas of your job. You might feel like it doesn't affect you much, but that's how many officers usually feel. Before you take comfort in that, consider the high suicide rate, high domestic violence rate, and other negatives of the job. Of course there are a variety of reasons that come in to play, but negativity and constant hypervigilance are huge factors. I recommend looking further in to the topic of hypervigilance, but basically your body and mind go through a lot from being constantly on high alert during work and then going home to a low state of being. Although you may not be able to tell what's going on, your body can and it reacts whether you acknowledge it or not. If you dismiss this idea, remember, science is real and it tends to be more reliable than an uneducated opinion.

Rather than maintain and foster a negative status quo with the population who dislikes you, be a part of the change. For your sake and theirs. Yes it will take work and patience, but so did coming to have more diverse police forces, yet here we are. None of the progress in policing was achieved by leaving difficult areas untouched or maintaining the status quo. Treating people with respect and being nice is important, but that's only a start. Imagine if you had a strong hate or fear of someone. Would you all of a sudden like them because they were nice to you once? Probably not. Work on building a rapport with them by addressing the elephant in the room. Don't do it in a sarcastic or demeaning tone either. Be sincere and show that you understand and can admit that their dislike for cops is valid. Then make it clear that you are putting forth the effort to make things different. You might initially be met with rudeness or no response, but people will start to think about it on their own time when their adrenaline isn't high. Maintain respect even when they're rude. Let them know, the same way they don't want to be judged based on their demographics, is the same way you don't want to be either. It goes both ways.

Don't make the mistake of downplaying whatever problem they mention they have with cops. For example, if they respond to you by saying how corrupt or racist cops are, don't try to sugar coat those facts. They believe it and it's a fact that corruption and racism are big problems in law enforcement. If your focus is on downplaying those facts rather than acknowledging they are problems, it shows you're more concerned with your image than with the actual harm caused by those issues. It also shows you are comfortable with the current amount of corruption and racism. You might feel like your department doesn't have those problems and that may be true, but your image is based on centuries of history, as well as other departments.

I briefly mentioned not using a sarcastic or demeaning tone, but tone will make or break you. There is a tendency to be "respectful" and "polite," but in a tone that directly undermines those behaviors. Using manners in a condescending tone is no different than outright being rude. The same way you can pick up on those tones toward you, people can hear you too. Being able to control your tone when emotions are high or you're not being respected is very hard to do, but it's a skill that practice will help improve. Gaining an understanding of and relating to the pain and harm law enforcement has caused people, will strongly help you in this area.

If you interact with minors from communities which dislike law enforcement, it's important that you discuss with them why their community feels that way, even if the kids seem to like you. As a kid who hated cops, there was a disconnect between my hate and the good cops I encountered. When they would do fun activities with us, I enjoyed the moment, but it stopped there. As soon as it was over, I was back in the streets still relating to "f*ck the police." Just like I wasn't thinking of hating police during the fun activity, I wasn't thinking of nice officers in our normal environment. They were two separate compartments in my brain. You have to make that connection for the kids you encounter. You have to deliberately say you are good, but people think you're bad because some cops are. Help them develop their critical thinking about their community and relationship with law enforcement. Make the most of their impressionable age because adults are much harder to get through to.

An Investment

Even if you became a cop because you needed a well paying job, you might as well make the most of your career. As I mentioned, you are a part of the community. Even if you're a hermit and avoid people at all costs on your off time, you still exist in the same world as everyone else. If you brought or will bring kids in to this world, they're a part of the community. Your loved ones are a part of the community. This means the strangers in this world have an affect on you at any given moment. Use this job to invest solutions to the problems that plague us all. Although the job of policing might feel like an investment in itself, it isn't much. Policing simply cleans up every time there is a problem. Imagine if you had a leak in your roof. Would you just keep cleaning the mess every time or would you try to fix the leak? Use your job to work on fixing our problems. If not for your sake, for the sake of your loved ones. The majority of street crime and troubles happen among people who were failed at home in some way and had little to no positives to help send them in a better direction. When a strong pattern like that exists, it's naive to think they're just inherently bad.

You changing the mentality toward law enforcement or just being a positive point of contact is a major investment. I was one kid from the hood who was able to overcome the cycle of poverty and whose mind changed about law enforcement, but that made one less criminal on the streets and I made it my mission to change the minds of others. Even if you only change a few minds, they will pass it on to their family unit and create other chain reactions. Yes you're one person, but change happens when one person does their part and it's added with the many other people doing their part. Sh!t adds up! If you've ever walked by an area where there was a lot of dog poop everywhere, you know this to be true. Someone didn't just drop a ton of poop there at once. One person not picking up their dog's poop was added to other people not picking up theirs. They didn't need to coordinate with each other or anything! Make your investment and let it add up with mine and everyone else's.

Self-Awareness & Emotional Intelligence

It's CRUCIAL for you to continuously develop your self-awareness and emotional intelligence.

They allow you to be aware of why you operate and give you the ability to react properly in scenarios. Most people assume they have self-awareness and emotional intelligence, however the opposite is true. I highly recommend exploring these topics on your own, but I'll shed some light on them. How to develop self-awareness and emotional intelligence differs depending on who you are. For me, it started when I had to write a college paper about personal prejudices. In writing about my behavior and how I was rude toward certain people, I came to the shocking realization I was racist. Obviously I was committing the behavior, but I never actually stopped to reflect on what I was doing and why. Actually putting it in to words and describing it really shined a light on how ridiculous and illogical I was. Especially since I knew first hand what it felt like to be on the receiving end of racism.

I started developing my self-awareness 12 years ago and I'm still learning new things about my everyday beliefs. Although it'll probably be an ongoing process, the point is that we remain open minded and not rigidly stuck in our ignorance. It's hard to question ideas you've always believed. A good way to start is by writing down all the random things you believe to be true about people from other demographics and your own and google if they're actually true. Also contemplate if it's logical for you to judge a whole population based on what you believe.

Another starting point is to consider what thoughts pop in your mind when you envision certain demographics. Compare how your actions and thoughts differ between groups you generally view favorably and groups you view unfavorably. Whether you can admit it out loud or not, as a human, your actions vary accordingly. This is why statistics show officers are more likely to stop, search, and cite brown people, despite white people offending at similar or higher rates. The only way to minimize such occurrences is to acknowledge your biases and deliberately counteract them. Whether we are aware or not, our brains operate automatically based on our biases and it's up to us to purposefully regulate it. While I was on duty I would continuously ask myself, 'would I act this way if this person was ___ (fill in the blank)?' I would also be mindful of the types of individuals who usually caught my attention and why. If you're convinced criminals tend to look a certain way, that means you're likely ignoring the ones who don't look that way, even when they're engaging in troublesome behavior.

In order to figure yourself out, you have to find the why's behind your actions and emotions. You have to be able to outright admit it to yourself. Don't downplay it, don't use roundabout language, or any other subtle form of avoidance. If you're unwilling to face what makes you uncomfortable, you won't make much progress in improving. You'll also remain sensitive in that area and highly provokable. Another way I developed my self-awareness and emotional intelligence was by considering the stereotypes about my own demographics and how I would feel if someone incorrectly assumed I fit them. Do you know the stereotypes about your demographics? Do they all apply to you and your peers?

A lack of emotional intelligence is a common reason behind misconduct and excessive use of force. The following are signs you may need to develop your emotional intelligence. This is going to be hard for some of you to read because it applies to you. If you're upset because something applies to you, that means you recognize you don't want to be that way. The best remedy is to focus on correcting the issue so it no longer applies to you. Don't focus on being upset that it was pointed out. Remember, no sugar coating or downplaying whatever applies.

- When you're having a bad day, you seek confrontation or lash out at others who are unrelated to your frustration.
- You enjoy provoking or belittling others.
- You take it personal when a victim's tone is escalated.
- You must retaliate against someone for disrespecting you.
- You get upset or physical when strangers insult you.
- You're unable to recognize or acknowledge when you're at fault or wrong.
- You use your position to inappropriately control people.
- You refuse to consider criticism or it highly upsets you.
- Your feelings usually outweigh anyone else's.
- You lack empathy.
- Your actions primarily depend on fitting in.

- You prefer to use violent tactics rather than deescalate.

Lessons From George Floyd's Case

Well. Here we are again dealing with riots over the same issue. This book was already completed before this case happened, but there are too many lessons here to not address them. Obviously there are a lot of strong emotions from all sides. From a law enforcement perspective, it would be best if you could understand this situation on a personal level, but if not, there are tactical and logical ways to understand it. First, that we're here AGAIN and FOR THE SAME REASON is ridiculous. That tells us law enforcement was placed in this predictable and preventable situation because of law enforcement behavior. To be clear, George Floyd's murder was the tipping point for an issue that was already brewing. Police brutality and misconduct are issues across the board. Like most societal issues, they disproportionately affect historically marginalized groups. Remember, it's not just the problematic officers who are to blame. It's also the ones who allow their behavior to continue.

The irony in this whole situation is, extreme and unjust policing tactics got us in this mess and yet, that was the first response many departments had to the peaceful protests (separate from the riots). Clearly the lesson was missed. Why show up with a negative view of people who are protesting injustice and bad policing? Good officers should also be against bad policing. As much as some officers stand by strong arm policing, studies continuously show it's counterproductive. This is not a new idea. I encourage you to explore how other countries, such as Finland and Canada, operate in policing and corrections. This is not to say force can't be used. The point is to use force only when necessary and to keep situations as minimal as possible. The departments who understood this concept did fine with their protests and were even socializing with the crowds. Protesting is a legal right we all have and there was no reason to show up with an aggressive mentality or posture. For the officers who feel otherwise, if we fail to recognize the role law enforcement played in this whole situation, we will find ourselves here again. It's similar to repeat offenders who keep getting arrested. Many of them can't understand why they keep having problems because they can't recognize their own destructive behavior. Officers are better than that.

As for the riots, there were different things at play. White extremists saw this as an opportunity to start the civil war they've been planning for years. I know this sounds far fetched for some people, but the FBI has been tracking them for years and is continuously thwarting their efforts. Some of the other rioters were opportunists and some wanted to return the hurt that law enforcement and society have always inflicted upon them. Although our initial reaction may be to denounce and dismiss them, their anger and disregard aren't without reason and are largely preventable as well. Ask yourself, why would so many people jump at the opportunity to inflict damage and chaos? It isn't normal for people to just want to hurt others and act out for no reason.

As someone from a harsh upbringing, I can relate to not giving a damn about society because I felt nobody gave a damn about me. I definitely didn't give a damn about any damage or problems caused to corporations. However, I also remember I wasn't initially that way as a kid. I always wanted to give things to people and help them. That slowly got chipped away by a negative home environment, disinterested school officials, and all the harshness that comes with impoverished neighborhoods. I didn't understand this until I studied college level psychology, sociology, and history.

America is a system of chain reactions. The more you study it, the more you recognize the society we see today is a direct product of events set in motion long ago, that have yet to be disrupted. Pick any social issue and you can trace it back to something beyond where the average person places blame. Some people think since a few have escaped whatever negative cycle they were in, more people just need to try harder. Of course this usually comes from people who never had to do that or who lack an understanding of how our system and psychology work. I compare such a response to thinking injured or murdered victims of a mass shooting should have just tried harder to escape. Other people escaped, why couldn't they?

With that said, I'll address common misperceptions. Many people incorrectly believe Black and Latino people offend at higher rates. The reality is, the greatest predictor of street crime is social status and poor Whites offend at similar rates. If you feel like your experience tells you otherwise, take a step back and reflect on why. First remember, studies and data weigh more than uneducated opinions and limited experiences. I strongly recommend you learn about our justice system and crime statistics. Although statistics are important, people often misinterpret them or see only a small portion of a much larger picture. Unless you're educated in this area, there are a lot of complexities and nuances you won't understand or know to look for on your own. I encourage you to not just rely on statistics, but actually read articles about them and explore cases.

Second, most low income neighborhoods have historically been populated by ethnic minorities because of racist practices, such as housing redlining. I encourage you to watch videos on this topic, but in a nutshell, White people deliberately made separate neighborhoods for minorities and marked them as bad simply because they were not White. They deliberately minimized the resources and services to minority neighborhoods and diverted them to White ones. They also prevented development from thriving and made it a point to reserve loans mainly for fellow White people. In other words, impoverished minority neighborhoods were a deliberate creation. If you only patrol minority low income neighborhoods, of course your experiences are going to be skewed. Whereas if you had a White low income neighborhood to compare it to, your experience would be different.

On a final note, reflect on the many ways the riots and protests impacted yours or other officer's lives. Higher threat levels, injured officers, impacted shifts, whole department buildings burned down, longer standing periods, an increase in negative encounters, loss of property, negatively affected loved ones, etc. Never forget these consequences and never forget the valuable lesson this teaches you about your authority. The reality is, law enforcement is greatly outnumbered and your authority exists because people let it by choosing to respect it. This is always taken for granted. Look how overwhelmed departments were with just a small fraction of people being involved. Let's aim to not have this happen again. Let's each do better and make sure our fellow officers do as well. If you keep doing what you've always done, you will keep getting the same results. If you want to avoid another mass scale uprising, you have to do something different. If you're religious, a good person, or just have good morals, you should naturally want to do things differently.

Contact: Helpvillage@outlook.com

Random Helpful & Reliable Sources:

Emotional Survival For Law Enforcement- Book by Kevin M. Gilmartin.

open.lib.umn.edu- Explains crime trends, discusses various social problems relevant to policing.

NPR.org- National Public Radio. News, true stories, investigative journalism, politics, brain games, and more.

APA.org- American Psychological Association. Research, help center resources, educational network, and more.

asanet.org- American Sociological Association. Studies, educational information, educator resources, journals, and more.

scholar.google.com- A search engine to find scholarly sources.

www.ingramcontent.com/pod-product-compliance
Lightning Source LLC
Chambersburg PA
BHW081100240526
65CB00025B/2800